DOMINIK EBERHARD

A Night in the Zoo

CORNELSEN
ENGLISH
LIBRARY

CORNELSEN **ENGLISH** LIBRARY

Dominik Eberhard · **A Night in the Zoo**

Verlagsredaktion
Stefan Höhne (Projektleitung); Ulrike Berendt, Gareth Evans *sowie* Sophia Schneider

Umschlaggestaltung
hawemannundmosch, Konzeption und Gestaltung, Berlin

Titelbild
Shutterstock/Danny Ye

Illustration
M. B. Schulz, Düsseldorf

Gestaltung & technische Umsetzung
L101 Mediengestaltung, Fürstenwalde

www.cornelsen.de

1. Auflage, 1. Druck 2020

Alle Drucke dieser Auflage sind inhaltlich unverändert und können im Unterricht nebeneinander verwendet werden.

Druck: H. Heenemann, Berlin

ISBN 978-3-06-035899-1

CONTENTS

1 LUKE MILLER

"Luke! Get up, now!"

Mrs Miller is almost shouting at her son, Luke. It is quarter to eight, and he is still lying in bed.

"How often do I have to tell you? You're late for school!"

5 Luke opens one eye and then closes it again. He knows it is time to wake up, but he just cannot keep his eyes open.

Suddenly, there is a loud roar! Not just any roar, but a very loud lion's roar! It is so loud that the windows are rattling.

Now Luke's eyes are wide open. He jumps out of his bed
10 and grabs his binoculars. Then he looks out of his bedroom window. At first, he can only see some monkeys. They are running around, and some of them are climbing trees. But then, about forty metres from the monkeys, he can see the lion, the very big lion! And he is roaring again.

15 "Good morning, King Tut," Luke says and puts down his binoculars. "Time for breakfast, isn't it?"

Luke dresses and walks downstairs to the kitchen. Then he has a quick breakfast before his mother takes him to school, like every morning.

20 For Luke, wild animals are something normal. No, he does not live in Africa. He lives in a zoo. His father is the director of Stockbridge Zoo, and their house is right in the middle of it. Until last month, it was Luke's secret, but now everybody in his class knows. Luke does not really like that.
25 A lot of children now ask him if they can come and visit him. Luke thinks that some of them only want to do that because they want to visit the zoo without a ticket. But his best friend

Jeff is not like that. He is already waiting for Luke at the school gate. Luke and Jeff are in Year 7 at Stockbridge School, and they are in the same class.

"Hi, Luke! Are you all right?"

"Yeah, just a bit tired. Mum doesn't like it when I'm late. 5 You know, I always need someone to wake me up. This morning, it was King Tut."

Suddenly, a girl comes towards the two boys.

"Hey, Luke, how are your monkeys? Do they still like playing with you? I'm sure they do. You're the perfect friend 10 for them."

"Yes, the monkeys are fine," Luke replies with a funny look on his face. "Thanks for asking. Oh, and Suzie is fine too. Only she was a bit hungry this morning. Maybe you want to ask your brother Robbie to come and feed her after school?" 15

"Oh, shut up!" the girl shouts. Then she turns around and walks away. Jeff starts to laugh.

"That was cool, Luke. She is such a cow! And her brother Robbie isn't any better. I mean, isn't that silly? He and his friends are the Snakes gang, but when he gets the chance to 20 touch a real snake, Suzie, he's too scared to hold her! And he doesn't even know what snakes eat.'

"Yeah, it's good that Robbie leaves me alone now," says Luke. "But I still feel like a celebrity. I really don't like that. And too many people want to visit the zoo for free now. But 25 my parents don't want that. They say we need the money for the animals!"

"That's true. I can understand that," Jeff replies. "So, what are you going to do in the summer holidays?"

"Guess what," says Luke. "I'm going to help my parents in the zoo. There's always a lot of work to do. What about you?"

"Well, we're going to visit my aunt in Cornwall for a few days. They live in Plymouth."

5 "Oh no, don't you get a lot of rain there?" asks Luke.

"No, you don't," replies Jeff. "It's often sunny, and there are some beautiful beaches. Maybe we're going to go sailing too. But the best thing is: my cousin is going to celebrate his birthday – at Plymouth Aquarium!"

10 "Really? So you're going to have fish and chips for lunch, I guess."

"Very funny!" says Jeff. "Listen, no lunch, because it's going to be a sleepover."

"A sleepover at the aquarium? Cool! How does that work?" 15 asks Luke.

"Well, they only do four sleepovers every year, in the school holidays. We arrive at seven in the evening. First, we watch a film about sea life and the work they do there. Then there is a tour of the aquarium, where you can see what fish 20 do at night. And we can watch the feeding of the sharks! There are also some games, midnight snacks and breakfast in the café."

"But where are you going to sleep?" Luke asks.

"Justin says we're going to sleep in our sleeping bags in 25 front of an aquarium window. I'm really looking forward to it!"

"Yes, sounds really exciting," says Luke. "Almost like the birthday parties at our zoo."

"I like your zoo," a voice suddenly says. There is a boy 30 standing right next to Luke and Jeff.

"Oh, hello, Jacob," the two boys say together. Jacob is one of their classmates.

"Sorry to ask you, Luke," says Jacob. "A friend is going to visit me next week. Do you think you could get us a free ticket for the zoo?" 5

Luke looks at Jeff and sighs.

2 A NEW IDEA

It is half past three. Mrs Miller is waiting in front of Stockbridge School. Luke says goodbye to his friend, Jeff, and then gets into his mum's car.

"Hello, love. How was school today?" Mrs Miller asks. 10

"All right," says Luke and looks out the window. He does not really want to talk. Mrs Miller understands her son and does not ask any more questions. But five minutes later, she tries again.

"Are you OK? Or are you still angry about that stupid boy 15 – what's his name?"

"Robbie," Luke replies. "No, he leaves me alone now. But his sister, Dana, is a silly cow ..." They are already back in the zoo. "This morning she ... oh, look, there's Tom!"

Suddenly, Luke is smiling and his mum stops. He opens 20 the car window and shouts at a person in a red "SZ" T-shirt and a black cap.

"Tom! Wait for me! I want to help you feed the otters!"

Luke opens the car door and jumps out. Then he turns to his mother in the car. 25

"Mum, can I go with Tom?"

"What about your homework?" Mrs Miller replies. "You know the rule: homework comes before the animals."

"There's not much homework today," Luke says. "And also, when I'm older, I want to be a zookeeper, just like Tom."

5 "But you are already a zookeeper, love," Mrs Miller says. "You are part of the zoo team."

"Oh, come on, Mum! Please!"

"All right, all right," Mrs Miller sighs. "But not in your school uniform. Go and get your zoo clothes and be home by 10 six."

"Cool, thanks, Mum!"

"Let's meet at the otters in ten minutes, Tom," Luke shouts and runs off to their house.

Ten minutes later, Tom is waiting for Luke at the otter 15 pool. The four otters are already excited because they know it is feeding time. They are swimming around and making funny sounds. There is an old basket full of dead fish next to Tom. After five more minutes, Luke arrives at the pool.

"Sorry I'm late, Tom," Luke says. "It's just because of my 20 school uniform. It's so stupid that I always have to change my clothes after school. Why do we have to wear this stupid uniform, anyway?"

Tom laughs.

"Why don't you go to Germany?" he says. "They don't 25 have to wear school uniforms there."

"They don't?" Luke asks and looks at Tom. "How do you know?"

"My nephew lives there."

"Your nephew is German?" Luke asks with his eyes wide open.

"Well, half German," says Tom. "My sister is married to a German. They live somewhere near Cologne. My nephew, Ron, is about your age. You can meet him next week because they're going to visit us in England. He wants to see what I do here at the zoo." 5

Luke does not say anything. He does not really like the idea of another boy at the zoo. What if Ron wants to be a zookeeper too? What if he wants to help Tom all the time? 10 Luke grabs a dead fish and throws it into the pool.

"Yeah, I'd like to meet him," Luke says. "Let's see if he also likes to feed dead animals to the otters."

An hour later, Luke's mobile phone rings. It is time for Luke to go home. And another hour later, the Miller family is 15 sitting around the dinner table. Mr Miller is looking a bit tired. "What about Omar?" Luke asks his father. "Is he feeling better?"

"Yes, the elephants are fine now," Mr Miller says. "But yesterday, two of the monkeys were sick. I had to call the vet 20 again."

"They're going to be fine too, Dad, aren't they?" Megan says. Megan is Luke's little sister. She is eight years old.

"Sure," says Mr Miller. "But the vet is expensive. And there were not so many visitors in the last three months." 25

Luke suddenly remembers Jacob.

"Erm, Dad, could I have two free tickets?" he asks. "It's for a classmate and his friend."

Mr Miller looks at Luke and sighs.

"Luke, I'm sorry. It's not a good time now. I'm just telling everybody in the family that we have a little problem at the moment because there aren't enough visitors. Now, for me it's OK if one or two of your friends visit the zoo for free. But don't you think this is getting a bit too much?"

"Yeah," Luke says and looks down. "Sorry, Dad."

"Why don't we try to think of some new ideas about how to make the zoo more attractive?" Mrs Miller says. "What about our website? Maybe I can change a few things and make it more interesting. We can think about something interesting and new. And we can also use a lot more social media to tell people what they can do or see in our zoo. People always like what we do at the Learning Centre, or the birthday parties, but I don't think that too many people know about it."

"Good point," Mr Miller says. "And maybe we need something that makes us a bit different from all the other zoos. You know, something that people are going to talk about on social media."

"I have an idea!" Megan suddenly shouts out. "Let's do an elephant race! People could sit on Raj, Sheba, and maybe even Omar, and then we let them run down the safari path. See who gets to the monkeys' cage first. Visitors could win a prize, like a free ticket."

"That's a very nice idea, Megan," Mrs Miller says. "But don't you think it could be a bit dangerous? I mean, people could fall off the elephants, or the elephants could run the wrong way and hurt some other visitors."

Luke starts to smile. Megan does not say anything. She is looking a bit angry now.

Suddenly Luke remembers Jeff's holiday in Plymouth. "Hmm," he says. "I'm not sure, but what about a sleepover?"

"A sleepover?" Mr Miller asks and looks at Luke. "How does that work?"

"Well," Luke replies, "They do these things at Plymouth Aquarium. People really love it. We could, for example, do something in the Learning Centre and sleep there. But before, we could walk around the zoo at night, see what the animals do. That can be interesting because not all of our animals sleep at night."

"Well, that sounds really interesting," says Mrs Miller. "It could be the birthday party everyone wants to talk about."

"Yeah, we could start with our usual birthday show, you know, Suzie and all this, and later do a tour of the zoo with Tom," Luke says. He's looking excited now.

"There could be some games too, and maybe a midnight snack in the restaurant. People just have to bring their sleeping bags and some torches."

"Hmm," Mr Miller says. "I'm beginning to like the idea. But we have to talk to Tom first. See what he thinks. And, of course, we have to test it before we start to offer it."

"Great!" Luke shouts. "I can ask some of my friends. I'm sure we can do a test sleepover next week. It's the summer holidays."

"I want to be at the sleepover too," Megan says and smiles at Luke. Luke rolls his eyes.

"Right," Mrs Miller says, "let's write down some ideas for a great sleepover programme!"

3 TOM'S NEPHEW

"Can I come too?" a boy in a green T-shirt asks.

"Oh no, we're going to go away on holiday next week!" another boy says.

"Can I hold Suzie, Luke?" a girl called Ella asks and looks
5 at Luke.

It is the last day before the holidays, and Luke is standing in the middle of a small group of children at the school gate.

"Listen, this is only going to be a test," Luke says. "Maybe we're going to do more sleepovers after that. But at the
10 moment we can only start with seven people. So that's Jeff and me, of course, and Ella. Sorry, Jacob, I don't have a free ticket for you and your friend, but you can both join us for the sleepover."

"Yes!" Jacob shouts out loud.

15 "That only makes five people," the boy in the green T-shirt says. "So, can I come too?"

"I'm sorry, Paul," Luke replies, "but there's also Ron, Tom's nephew from Germany. That makes seven. I'm sure you can do it next time."

20 "A German?" Paul says with a strange look on his face. "Can he understand what you're talking about at the zoo?"

"Tom says his English is very good," Luke says. "Most Germans are not so bad at languages. Well, better than us, I think. Or how good is your German, Paul?"

25 "Sorry, Luke," Jacob says. "But the Germans in the films my father always watches are often a bit stupid."

"Those are just stupid films," Luke replies.

"Well, all I can say is that it's a silly language," Ella says. "My brother in Year 10 is doing German. It's so difficult! You know, they have so many different words for 'the' – they're mad!"

"All right," Luke says. "Once again: language is not a 5 problem here. And Tom is our zookeeper. He's going to show us around the zoo, so I can't say that his nephew can't be there."

Then Luke looks at Paul.

"I'm sorry, Paul," he says. "Maybe my little sister is going 10 to be there too, so we're really enough people. Next time?"

"All right, then," Paul says. "No problem, I have to go now. Have fun, all of you."

"OK, everyone," Luke says. "There's my mum. See you next Saturday, at seven o'clock. And don't forget your 15 torches!"

Later in the afternoon, Luke is helping Tom again. They are cleaning the rhesus monkeys' cage. Tom holds a piece of banana out to one of the monkeys. The monkey first looks at the banana, then at Tom. 20

"Come here, Luis," Tom says in a soft voice. "Fresh banana. Mmm, yummy!"

The monkey takes a step towards Tom. Then another step. Suddenly, he grabs the piece of banana from Tom, turns around and climbs up a tree. Another monkey comes 25 running towards Luis. But before he can take the banana away from him, Luis puts it into his mouth. The other monkey makes an angry sound, a loud 'screech, screech'.

"It's good that Luis and Charly are feeling better now," Luke says. 30

"Yes, the vet's really great," Tom says. "He only has a bit too much work with our animals at the moment."

"So, what do you think about the sleepover programme, Tom?" Luke asks.

5 "It's good," Tom replies. "I think it's a great idea. And I think we can do it."

"Can my friends also feed the tigers?" Luke asks. "Or maybe the lions? You know, they're very active at night."

"Hmm, I'm not sure," Tom says. "You know that it's not so 10 easy. King Tut doesn't like it when other people get too near to the fence. And the lions often fight for the food. I think it's a bit too dangerous. You know, King Tut can get very angry."

"All right," Luke says. "It's fine just to watch you do it. But what about the monkeys? Can we go into the monkey's cage 15 at the sleepover?" Luke sounds excited. "Well, I don't know. We can't usually do that, of course. But for this sleepover, let's see what your friends are like, OK? I think we already have a really good programme, Luke," Tom says. "Anyway, let's go to the otters now. I have a text message from Ron. 20 He's waiting for us there."

Suddenly, Luke remembers Ron. Now he is here, and Luke is going to meet him. Luke does not really want to, but he cannot say 'no'. Tom is the boss now.

Luke picks up their cleaning things and puts them in a 25 big bag. Then he walks over to the door of the cage. He makes sure that no monkey is following him. Luke waits for a moment, opens the door and walks out of the cage. The he closes the door fast. Tom takes the other things and follows Luke the same way.

From far away, Luke can see a boy in a white T-shirt. The boy is watching the otters. He looks like he is having fun. Suddenly, the boy takes something out of a basket and throws it into the otter pool. The otters make their funny 'eeep-eeep' sounds. They are having fun too. 5

"Is he feeding our otters?" Luke says and looks at Tom. He cannot believe what he sees.

"Yes," Tom says. "I think he can help us a little bit, can't he?"

Luke does not reply. He is feeling very strange now. 10

"Hey, Ron!" Tom shouts. "Come here and say hi to Luke!"

Ron turns around and smiles. Then he walks towards Luke.

"Hiya! How're you doing?" Ron says to Luke. "I'm Ron. Nice to meet you." 15

"Erm, nice to meet you too," Luke says after a moment. He is surprised at Ron's English: it sounds perfect!

"Uncle Tom says you're his partner. I hope it's fun working with him. I know my uncle can give people a hard time!" Ron looks at Tom and laughs. Tom is smiling. 20

"So you're from Cologne?" Luke asks.

"Yeah. Well, we live in a small town called Pulheim. I'm sure you don't know it. It's not very far from Cologne, maybe about ten kilometres. We often go into Cologne at the weekend, to go shopping. It's a great city. And they have a 25 great zoo too."

"Do they?" Luke asks.

"Yes. I really like it. They also have a small aquarium next to the zoo, and two other buildings with insects and reptiles.

But the zoo in Duisburg is even better. They have some giant otters. They're really interesting."

"I see," Luke says. "I guess they're not like our boring little ones here."

5 "Oh no," Ron says. "I really like the little ones. They're so cute. And Stockbridge Zoo looks like a great zoo too."

"So, do you want to be a zookeeper when you're older?" Luke asks.

"A zookeeper? Not really," Ron says. "I'm just interested in
10 animals. I love animals. Well, not all animals. I do not like spiders."

"I love animals too," Luke says and smiles. "But I do not like wasps."

"Them too," Ron says. "Spiders and wasps."

15 The two boys laugh.

"Your English is really good," Luke says. "How come?"

"Well, my mother's English, of course," Ron replies. "She's Tom's sister. I only speak English with her. And I speak German with my father and my friends."

20 "Wow, that's great," Luke says. "You can speak two languages!"

"Yeah. For me it's normal. But at school I sometimes feel like a celebrity. My friends often come and ask me, "What's this in English?" and "How do you say that in English?" Even
25 my English teacher sometimes asks me things, like, "Ron, you're a native speaker. Can you say that?"

Luke looks at Ron.

"I think I know how you feel," Luke says.

"What do you mean?" Ron asks.

"Well, nothing," Luke replies. "It's just that some of the other children think it's funny that I live in a zoo."

"Don't worry," Ron says. "They're just jealous."

"So, what's your school like?" Luke asks.

"It's OK," Ron replies. "I guess it's just like a normal German school. It's probably the same as your school. We have lessons in the morning. Then we have lunch in our canteen. And in the afternoon, there are often activities, or we get help with our homework."

"Is it true that you don't have school uniforms in Germany?" Luke asks.

"Yes, that's true. We can usually wear what we want. But we can't wear costumes, of course." Ron laughs. "Only at carnival."

"Sounds great," Luke says. "Now it's me who's jealous. I don't like school uniforms. It's so much better if you can wear what you want."

"Well, yes and no," Ron says. "It can also be a problem. Some children always wear very expensive clothes. Children who don't have so much money feel bad about that. And with a uniform, you don't have to think about what to wear when you get up in the morning, so you can sleep longer. I think a school uniform isn't such a bad idea."

"Sorry to interrupt you, boys!" Tom suddenly says. "But the otters are waiting for their food."

"Sorry, Tom," Luke says. "Come on, Ron, let's give them some yummy dead fish."

"Good idea," Ron says, and the two boys walk over to the otter pool.

4 THE BIG NIGHT

It is very quiet at Stockbridge Zoo. Sometimes you can hear an animal making a sound from a far corner of the zoo. The zoo closes at six, and now it is about half past six on a Saturday evening. There are no more visitors. But there is a man and a young boy. They are walking along the main road 5 towards a house in the middle of the zoo. The man is carrying a rucksack. The boy is holding a video camera. Sometimes he stops in front of a cage and films with it. After a few minutes, they arrive at the house. The door opens, and Luke comes out. 10

"Hey, Jeff!" Luke shouts.

"Hi," Jeff says and looks at Luke. "Are you all right?" he asks.

"Yes," Luke replies. "A bit nervous, but fine. Oh, hello, Mr Sammon." 15

"Hello, Luke," Jeff's father says. "We're a bit excited too. But I'm sure it's going to be a great sleepover."

Then Mrs Miller comes out too.

"Hello, Alex," she says. "Would you like a cup of tea? Do come in, please." 20

"Thanks, but I have to go," Mr Sammon replies. "Joanne's waiting in the car at the zoo gate. Anyway, the children want to be on their own now, don't they?"

"That's right," Mrs Miller says and smiles.

Mr Sammon gives Jeff the rucksack. 25

"Right. You have your sleeping bag and your torch?" he asks.

"Yes, Dad," Jeff replies and rolls his eyes.

"Good," he says. "See you tomorrow morning, ten o'clock. And thanks for everything, Barbara. Bye!" Then Mr Sammon walks off.

"So, how was Plymouth?" Luke asks Jeff.

5 "It was great," Jeff replies. "The sleepover was really good. The best thing was feeding the sharks! Are we going to feed some animals too? The lions, maybe?"

"Yes," Luke replies, "but not the lions. Tom's going to do that. We're only allowed to feed the rhesus monkeys. But 10 maybe we can go into the cage!"

"Yeah! I'm sure they're more exciting than lions and sharks, anyway." Jeff says and laughs. But then he stops when he sees Luke's face.

"So, you have a video camera?" Luke asks.

15 "Oh, yes," Jeff says. "That's my new hobby. My cousin, Justin, has one too. We had a lot of fun making short films. He's really good at it. And he sometimes edits the films and uploads them on the internet."

"Really?" Luke says. "That sounds fun."

20 "It is," Jeff says. "His next project is going to be a kung fu film. It's called 'Master Wu and the magic book'."

"Wow, when are we going to see that at the cinema?" Luke laughs. But when he sees Jeff's face, he stops.

"Anyway," Luke goes on, "maybe you can make a great 25 film of our sleepover. I'm sure we can use it for our website."

"Good idea," Jeff says and smiles again.

It is quarter past seven now. All the sleepover children are in the Learning Centre: Luke, Jeff, Ron, Ella, Jacob and his friend Malik. Tom is there too. They are waiting for Mrs

Miller to arrive. In the back of the room, there are lots of rucksacks and sleeping bags. Malik is already holding his torch.

"So, is that the German boy?" Ella whispers to Luke and points to Malik. 5

"No, I'm the German boy," Ron says. He is standing next to Luke. "Nice to meet you."

"Errr, but you sound very English," Ella says. Her face is getting red.

"Really?" Ron replies and makes a funny face. "Must be 10 the English breakfast I had this morning."

"Oh no, here she comes ... my little sister," Luke suddenly says. Megan comes into the room together with their parents. Then Megan joins the other children and smiles at Luke.

"Hello and good evening, everyone," Mrs Miller says. 15 "Welcome to our first sleepover here at Stockbridge Zoo. We're going to start with our little show and some information about dangerous animals. After that, Tom is going to give you a tour of the zoo. That's when you need your torches. You don't need them now." 20

Mrs Miller looks at Malik.

"Oh, OK. Sorry," Malik says and puts his torch into his rucksack.

"Right," Mrs Miller goes on. "Later, we're going to have a midnight snack in the restaurant, so you don't have to eat 25 anything when you are with Tom. The food that he has is just for the animals, not for you anyway," she says and smiles.

The children laugh.

"Now, what do you think I have in this box?" Mrs Miller asks. 30

"I know!" Megan shouts out. Luke closes his eyes and sighs.

"Maybe a small alligator?" Jacob says.

"Not bad," Mrs Miller says. "It's not an alligator, but it's
5 also a reptile."

"A snake!" Ella shouts. "That must be Suzie!"

"Correct," Mrs Miller says and opens the box. Then she takes out Suzie and puts her around her neck.

"Oh my God!" Malik shouts. "It's an anaconda!"

10 "She's not an anaconda," Megan laughs. "She's a boa constrictor!"

"Hmm, are you sure about that?" Jacob says. "I mean, she really looks like the snakes in the films my father always watches. I'm sure that snake can eat you in one bite. So be
15 careful!"

"Now listen," Mrs Miller says. "Suzie is a boa, and she is only three metres long, so she can't eat you. She only eats mice and rats."

"Where does she come from?" Jeff asks.

20 "Suzie is from Mexico," Mrs Miller says. "She's eight years old and ..."

"Like me!" Megan shouts out.

Mrs Miller looks at her. "She's eight years old, like Megan, and she weighs twelve kilos, not like Megan."

25 The children laugh again.

"So, who would like to hold Suzie now?" Mrs Miller asks.

Suddenly, the room is quiet. Nobody says anything.

"I think Ella wants to," Luke says.

"Errr, yes, but I'm not so sure now," Ella says.

30 "Come on, it's fun!" Luke says.

Mrs Miller walks over to Ella.

"Maybe you want to touch her first," Mrs Miller says.

Ella puts her hand on the snake's back.

"It feels cold," she says.

"That's right," Mrs Miller says. "Reptiles don't have a high 5
body temperature. That's why they usually don't move very
much. Do you want to hold her?" Ella looks a bit scared, but
she nods. Mrs Miller takes Suzie and puts her around Ella's
neck. The snake starts to move a bit. Now Ella is looking
scared. Suzie moves her head up. She is very close to Ella's 10
head now. Ella does not move. Suddenly, Suzie pushes out
her black tongue near Ella's face.

"Take her away! Take her away!" Ella screams. "She's going
to eat me!"

"She can't eat you!" Megan shouts and laughs. 15

Mrs Miller takes Suzie and puts her back in the box. Ella
is still looking scared.

"That was great," Jacob says. "Can I hold her now?"

"I think Suzie needs a little break now," Mrs Miller says.
"She can get a bit excited when too many people hold her. 20
But I can tell you something about other snakes, scorpions
and insects."

"Cool," Malik says. "Can we touch the scorpions too?"

"You can't touch scorpions, stupid!" Jacob says. "They can
kill you!" 25

"We don't have any scorpions in the zoo, anyway," Megan
says. "Only a few spiders."

"Really?" Malik says. "Like the big Australian ones?"

"No spiders, please," Ron says. "I do not like spiders!"

Luke looks at Jeff. 30

"Jeff, are you really filming all this?" Luke asks.

"Yes," Jeff smiles and puts down his camera. "I already have some brilliant scenes!"

Mrs Miller sighs. "OK, well, maybe it's a good idea to start
5 the tour now," she says and looks at Tom.

"Erm ... all right," Tom replies. "Then let's start now. Everybody please get your rucksacks and torches. We're going to visit the monkeys now. Just follow me. Let's go!"

5 THE RHESUS MONKEYS

It is eight o'clock in the evening, but it is not really dark
10 yet. The children are on their way to the monkeys' cage. Tom stops and turns to the children.

"Right," Tom says. "Some of us are going to go into the monkeys' cage in a minute. Rhesus monkeys sleep at night, so it's about bedtime for them now. But I still have a few
15 snacks for them."

Tom opens his rucksack and gives each kid some apples and bananas.

"Monkeys like fruit very much, but they eat almost everything that we do," Tom goes on. "Our little group here is
20 usually friendly, and they're not scared of us, but let's not make them angry with our torches. There's still enough light, anyway." The children put their torches into their rucksacks.

"Can we also go into the cage?" Ella asks.

"No, sorry, we can't all go in, but maybe two of you. The
25 monkeys don't like too many visitors. Now, before we go inside, we should try to show them that we're friends, so let's

first give them a piece of apple through the bars of the cage. Who wants to try?"

"Me!" Jacob shouts. "I want to do that!"

"All right," Tom says. "Come along with me. And the others please stay where you are." 5

The children watch as Jacob and Tom go towards the cage.

"OK," Tom says to Jacob. "Where's your apple?"

"Oh, sorry," Jacob replies. "It's in my rucksack."

Jacob puts down his rucksack next to the bars of the cage, 10 opens it, and takes out an apple. Some of the monkeys are watching him. They understand what is happening and start to walk towards the bars. One of the monkeys is carrying a baby monkey on her back. Suddenly, the baby monkey jumps onto a tree and watches everything. 15

"Oh, look!" Jeff shouts. "A baby monkey! How cute!"

"She's called Rosie," Megan says to Jeff. "She's three months old now. She's really the star of the group. And I sometimes play with her."

The monkeys are really close to the bars now. Jacob is 20 holding a piece of apple through the bars. One monkey comes towards him, grabs the piece of apple from him and runs away. More monkeys are coming towards him now.

"It works," Jacob says and smiles. "Come here. I have more fruit for you. I'm your friend." 25

Suddenly a monkey puts his hand into Jacob's rucksack, grabs his torch and runs away with a loud 'screech, screech'.

"Hey, what are you doing with my torch?" Jacob shouts. He's looking very angry now. "Give it back to me!"

The other children laugh. 30

"I think it's time to go into the cage now," Tom says and smiles. "But I can only take two people with me. So, who would like to join me?"

Both Jeff and Malik look down.

5 "Can I go?" Ella says and smiles. "I like monkeys more than snakes."

"I want to go too," Jacob says. "Maybe I can find my torch. And anyway, the monkeys know me now."

"Me too," Megan suddenly shouts. "All the monkeys know 10 me, so that shouldn't be a problem."

Tom thinks for a moment.

"All right," he says. "But only because you're a member of the zoo, Megan. So follow me, please. And don't forget your rucksack, Jacob."

15 Tom opens the door to the cage and lets Ella, Jacob and Megan in. He makes sure that no monkey is too close to the door. Then he closes the door behind him. The other children are watching them from outside the cage.

Jacob looks around the cage. "I want my torch back!" he 20 suddenly says. He is still angry. "Look! That one has it!"

High up on a tree, too high for Jacob, the monkey is playing with Jacob's torch.

"Hey, this is my last warning," Jacob shouts. "Give it back! Now!"

25 "Come on, Jacob," Jeff laughs. "Climb the tree!"

"Maybe you should just be nice to him," Tom says and gives Jacob another apple. But suddenly, the light of the torch goes on. The monkey screams and drops the torch. Jacob jumps onto the torch and grabs it. Then he looks at Jeff.

30 "Don't film that," Jacob says, but Jeff is only smiling.

"OK, stop it now! It's feeding time," Tom says.

The children inside and outside the cage take out their apples and bananas and hold some pieces towards the monkeys. Some monkeys take them without running away
5 now. Suddenly, a monkey jumps onto Jacob's back.

"Help!" Jacob shouts. "Help me, someone!"

All the children start to laugh.

No. Not all the children. Ella is not looking. Rosie, the baby monkey, is really close to her now. Rosie is not scared.
10 She takes some more small pieces of apple from Ella and puts them in her mouth. Ella opens her rucksack to get more fruit, but Rosie cannot wait. She climbs into Ella's rucksack. Ella cannot believe it. Rosie is inside now, and she likes it in there! Ella closes her rucksack and looks around. The other
15 children are still laughing. Jeff is filming Jacob with a monkey on his back. Only Megan is looking at Ella.

"Shush", Ella whispers to Megan. "I have a plan."

"What is it?" Megan asks.

"Let's take Rosie with us to the Learning Centre," Ella
20 whispers. "Then she can sleep with us. We can take her back to the cage tomorrow. But don't tell anybody."

"But we can't do that," Megan says. "The monkeys are not allowed to leave the cage!" She is looking worried.

"Come on, Megan, are you a little baby, like Rosie? I don't
25 like baby girls." Ella turns around and looks the other way.

"All right," Megan whispers back. "Let's do it."

The two girls smile at each other.

"OK everybody," Tom says. "I think that's enough for today. The monkeys are getting tired. And when they're tired,
30 they can sometimes get angry. So let's go to the otters now."

"That was fun, wasn't it?" Jeff says to Jacob, but Jacob does not reply.

Tom helps the three children leave the cage one after the other. Then he closes the door and smiles at the monkeys. They are really quiet now. Some of them are already sleeping. 5 Only one of the monkeys is still running around, looking for something.

Now it is almost dark in the zoo. All of the children are using their torches on the way to the otter pool. The zoo looks a bit scary now. There are a few lamps along the main 10 path, but they do not give very much light. The children can see that there are cages, but they cannot see the animals inside before they point their torches at them.

Suddenly, there is a loud roar!

"Wow!" Jacob shouts. "Are these the tigers?" 15

"This is King Tut, our biggest lion," Luke says. "I think he's still hungry."

"Yeah, but we're not allowed to feed him," Jeff says.

"Who wants to feed such a monster, anyway?" Malik says. "I'm sure he could bite your arm off if you try!" 20

"That's why you're not allowed to do it," Tom says. Then he turns to the other children. "OK, we're almost at the otter pool. We have four otters. Their names are Mickey, Minnie, Pip and Pop. They're from Asia, and they're very active at night. We have some light at the pool, but you can use your 25 torches to see them better."

The children are now standing around the pool. The otters look very excited. They make their loud 'eeep-eeep' sounds. Then they swim around in circles, jump out of their pool and roll around in the sand.

"That's a great show," Jeff says to Luke and looks through his camera. "And this is going to be a great video! But Luke,
5 don't you have four otters? I can only see three."

Luke takes a closer look now. There's Minnie, Mickey and Pop. But where is Pip?

"Tom! Tom!" Luke shouts.

"What's up, my friend?" Tom replies as he walks over to
10 Luke.

"Where's Pip?" Luke asks Tom. "I can't see him!"

"Give me your torch, please," Tom says to Luke. He sounds a bit worried.

Tom moves the torch up and down the pool. The other
15 three otters are still swimming around. Suddenly, he can see Pip in a corner next to the pool. The otter does not move. Is he dead? Then Pip opens his eyes and closes them again. But he still does not move.

"Oh no, not again!" Tom says. "Listen, Luke, Pip's sick. I
20 have to call the vet. And we have to be quick! Can I leave you here with your friends for a few minutes?"

"Yes, sure, Tom, no problem!" Luke says, but he's a bit nervous. Tom turns to the children.

"Listen, everyone. You stay here with Luke, OK? I only
25 need a few minutes," Tom says and leaves the children. He runs towards the main building. Luke does not know what to say.

"What's wrong?" Ron asks Luke.

"Pip's sick, and Tom's going to call the vet," Luke replies.
30 "We have to wait here."

"Erm, I can't wait here," Jacob says. "I have to get my rucksack. It's still in the monkeys' cage."

Luke looks at Jacob with wide open eyes. Then he opens and closes his mouth, but he can't say anything.

"Sorry, Luke," Jacob says and looks down. 5

"OK, why don't you two go and get it, and I can take care of the others here?" Ron says and smiles.

"Right," Luke says. "Good idea. Let's do that. And let's be quick before Tom comes back. Thanks, Ron!"

Then Luke and Jacob run off into the night. 10

"How can you be so stupid?" Luke says to Jacob with an angry look on his face. "You're really lucky that I have a key to the cage!"

Luke opens the door to the monkeys' cage, and the two boys go in. It is very quiet. They look around with their 15 torches.

"There it is!" Jacob suddenly says. He can see his rucksack lying on the ground. All the things that were in it are lying on the ground too.

"These stupid monkeys!" Jacob shouts out loud. "Wait 20 until I get you!"

"Don't get the monkeys, get your things!" Luke says. "We don't have much time!"

Jacob collects the things on the ground and puts them into his rucksack. Then Luke opens the door of the cage for 25 Jacob. Suddenly, something is moving behind Jacob. He turns around. One of the monkeys is coming towards him.

"I'm sure it was you!" Jacob shouts and points his torch at the monkey. The monkey makes a loud 'screech' sound and runs past Jacob, through the open door and out of the cage into some nearby bushes.

Luke cannot believe his eyes. He is feeling really sick.

"Oops," says Jacob. "Sorry, Luke."

5   "Tom's going to kill me!" Luke says. He is looking really scared now. Jacob does not say anything. The two boys are walking back to the otter pool.

"What are we going to do now?" Luke asks. "We can't tell Tom, that's for sure."

10   "Well, we have to catch the monkey before Tom finds out," Jacob says.

"Brilliant idea!" Luke says and gives Jacob a funny look. "And how are we going to do that?"

When Luke and Jacob arrive back at the otter pool, Ron is 15 talking to Malik. Jeff is filming the otters. Ella and Megan are talking to each other. Two men are coming towards the otter pool. It's Tom and the vet. They climb down the pool area and have a closer look at Pip. All the other children are watching them.

20   "It doesn't look too good," the vet says to Tom. "We have to take him to the Vet Centre. I can give him an injection, but then we have to watch him and see how he reacts."

"OK, let's do that," Tom says.

Together, the two men carry Pip out of the pool area.

25   "Great," Jeff says. "Then I can film some brilliant scenes at the Vet Centre."

"No way!" Tom says, and he sounds a bit angry. "Nobody is coming with us. The Vet Centre is not for children. Luke, I'm going to be away for maybe an hour or so. Go to the restaurant, please. We want to have a break in half an hour anyway, so you can start having snacks with your parents. I'm going to meet you there."

"All right, Tom," Luke says. He is still looking a bit scared when Tom and the vet carry Pip away. Then he turns to the other children.

"OK," Luke says. "So, let's all go to the restaurant."

"But what about the lions?" Jeff says. "I want to film them at night."

"Yeah," Malik joins in. "Let's see them first and then go to the restaurant."

"Sorry, I don't want to interrupt you," Ella says. "But Megan and I are going to go back to the Learning Centre right now."

She turns to Megan and winks at her.

"Yeah," Megan says. "We want to unpack our sleeping bags now. See you later at the restaurant!"

"But Megan," Luke says. "You can't do that! Tom wants us to go to the ..."

"I know what I can do!" Megan shouts. "I'm not a baby! Come on, Ella, let's go."

Then the two girls walk away.

"So, are we going to see the lions now?" Jeff asks.

"OK," Luke says. "To tell you the truth: we're not going to visit the lions, and we're not going to go to the restaurant."

"Why not?" Ron asks.

"Well, we have a problem," Luke says. "A very big problem!"

6 GOING ON A SAFARI

"That's a joke!" Jeff says with wide open eyes.

"No, it isn't," Luke says. "A monkey is running around the zoo. And we have to catch him before Tom finds out."

"Maybe he's not in the zoo any more," Jeff says. "Can he climb the zoo walls?" 5

"I hope not," Luke says. He's looking really worried now.

"How can a monkey get out of that cage?" Malik asks. "I mean, the bars look really ..."

"These things just happen," Jacob interrupts him.

"Let's not talk about that," Luke says. "We have to find 10 him and catch him. Any ideas on how to do that?"

"Well, I still have some fruit," Ron says. "It looks like the monkeys really like that. With a piece of banana or apple we can maybe get close to him and then put him into a bag or a rucksack." 15

"Sounds like a plan," Luke says. "But we have to be very quiet. And we shouldn't be using our torches. The monkeys are scared of them, you know."

"Maybe we should go in two groups," Jacob says. "Then our chances of finding him are better." 20

"Yeah, let's do that," Luke says. "Ron, can you go together with Malik? Jacob and Jeff are coming with me."

"No problem," Ron says.

The boys take two rucksacks and get ready for the big safari. 25

"Right," Luke says. "We're going this way. Ron and Malik, please have a look at the other part of the zoo. But remember, really: there should be enough light from the lamps, so no torches please. If one group finds the monkey, call the others. And let's meet again at the Learning Centre in about half an hour, OK? Let's go!"

Luke, Jeff and Jacob walk off towards the Elephant House. Jeff is still holding his camera.

"This is so cool!" Jeff says. "Catching a monkey – I think your sleepover is so much better than the one in Plymouth!"

Luke does not say anything.

"Sorry again, Luke," Jacob says. "I mean, when I was in that cage, I ..."

"Sorry, could you two be quiet please?" Luke says with an angry voice. "This is not a game! And the monkey can hear us and run away."

There is a long moment of silence. Nobody says anything. It is so quiet in the zoo that it is almost scary. Suddenly, there is some noise coming from the Elephant House. It sounds like the elephants are having trouble.

"Our elephants aren't usually like that," Luke says to Jeff and Jacob. "Let's have a look!"

"So, there was nothing around the monkeys' cage," Malik says. "Where are we going to look now?"

"Let's go to the lions," Ron whispers. "And please keep your voice down."

Malik nods. The two boys walk along the safari path between the monkeys and the lions. Suddenly, Ron stops and holds a finger up in front of his mouth. Malik does not say anything. Ron points to a bush at the side of the path. The boys do not move. There is a sound coming from the bushes.

Malik looks at Ron. He is looking a bit scared now. Something is moving in the bushes. Malik takes his torch, but Ron gives him a sign not to use it. There is some light from the lamps along the path, but not enough to see what
5 is moving. Then the bush is quiet again. Ron takes a piece of banana from his rucksack and moves towards the bush. Malik follows him.

Suddenly, two bright eyes appear in the dark bush! Malik's heart almost stops. Ron is a bit scared too, but he does not
10 move. He holds out the banana. The eyes look at him, but they do not move. There is a moment of silence.

Then everything happens very fast. A light goes on. It is Malik's torch. The two eyes jump out of the bush and run past Ron down the safari path, making a loud 'miaow' sound.
15 The two boys take a deep breath.

"Stupid cat," Ron says.

"You know, Ron, there's one thing I still don't understand," Malik says. "If we really find the monkey, how are we going to catch him?"

20 Luke, Jeff and Jacob open the door to the Elephant House. It is almost dark inside. The elephants are still making a noise.

"What are they doing?" Luke asks.

"Look, the baby elephant is running in circles," Jeff says.
25 "Don't you have some light in here?"

Of course! Luke goes back to the door and turns on the main light.

The boys cannot believe their eyes.

A rhesus monkey is sitting on Omar's back, screaming. The baby elephant is trying to get him off his back. His parents, Raj and Sheba, are watching the scene. When Omar sees Luke, he stops and looks at him.

"Omar!" Luke shouts. "Easy! Everything is fine!" 5

The monkey looks at Luke too. Then he jumps off Omar's back and runs away from the elephants towards the door of the Elephant House.

Luke cannot move. He just watches everything. He almost feels like he is watching an interesting film at the 10 cinema.

"Close the door!" Jeff shouts to Jacob.

But it is too late. The monkey turns around and looks at the boys. Then he runs through the open door and towards the safari path. 15

"So this is the lions' area," Ron whispers. "Can you see King Tut over there? He's the boss of the other three lions. Lions are usually very active at night, so we have to be careful."

"Well, we're lucky that they have a big fence around their 20 area," says Malik. "I don't think anybody wants to hide in there, not even a stupid monkey. Come on, let's move on."

Suddenly, Ron's mobile phone rings. It is Luke.

"Listen, Ron," Luke says, "the monkey was in the Elephant House, but now he's outside again. Where are you?" 25

"We're right in front of the lions," Ron replies.

"OK, I think he's running towards you. Can you see him?"

Ron turns his head and looks down the safari path. He cannot see anything. But then, about fifteen metres away

from them, something is moving near the fence. Ron looks at Malik, and before he can say anything, Malik takes his torch and points it at the fence. There he is! The monkey looks at the two boys and screams. He tries to run away from
5 the light of the torch and climbs up the fence and into the lions' area.

Ron takes a deep breath.

"Yes, I can see him," Ron says to Luke. "He's with us. Or, to be more correct, he's with King Tut now."

10 Three minutes later, all the boys are standing at the lions' fence. They cannot hear the monkey. But the lions are quiet too.

"Why is the monkey in there?" Malik asks. "Is he stupid?"

"Our monkeys don't usually leave their cage, so he doesn't
15 know how dangerous this is," Luke replies. "If the lions find him, he's a dead monkey!"

"But how are we going to get him out?" Jacob asks. "You don't want to go in there, do you?"

"Of course not, stupid!" Malik replies.

20 "I really have no idea," Luke says and sighs.

Suddenly, there is a loud roar. It is King Tut! What's happening to the monkey? Malik wants to know and points his torch at the lions. He can see King Tut. He is looking at something. Malik moves his torch. About five metres away
25 from King Tut, the monkey is sitting in the grass. He is picking up something from the grass. He does not care about the lion. And it looks like he does not know how dangerous this is.

"Get your torches, all of you!" Malik suddenly shouts. "Quick! And point them at the monkey! I know he doesn't like that!"

The children all take their torches and point them at the monkey. The monkey looks their way, screams, and starts to run away. King Tut starts to run after him. The children hold their breath.

The monkey is screaming and running really fast. But King Tut is getting closer and closer. Then, at the very last moment, the monkey climbs up a tree near the fence before the lion can get him.

King Tut does not try to climb the tree, but he looks at the monkey and gives him a loud roar. More lions are joining him now. Together, they walk around the tree. The monkey cannot get down any more. He is looking really scared now. He starts to move along the big branch that he is sitting on. The branch begins to go down, but the monkey does not stop moving. Suddenly, he jumps off the branch and grabs the top of the fence. Then he climbs down the fence to safety. He takes a quick look at the boys and runs off towards the main building.

"That was close," Jeff says. "I hope there was enough light for the video."

"Jeff, can you please stop worrying about your video?" Luke says. "We still have a big problem here!"

"You know what, Luke?" Jacob says. "I don't think we have a chance. We're never going to catch that monkey. Maybe we should just give up."

Luke looks at his friends. Nobody says anything.

"All right," Luke says. "Let's go back to the Learning Centre then. Maybe we have to tell Tom. And thanks, anyway. All of you."

7 HOW TO CATCH A MONKEY

"Isn't she cute?" Ella says. "Look how she's holding my finger!"

"She always does that," Megan says. "When I play with her, she sometimes even jumps on my back!"

Ella, Megan and Rosie, the baby monkey, are in the Learning Centre. The girls are sitting on the floor on their sleeping bags. Rosie is not in Ella's rucksack any more. She is sitting between Ella's legs, looking a bit nervous, or even scared. The girls want to give her an apple, but she doesn't move. It is her first time outside the cage, and she does not know where her mother is.

Suddenly, the girls can hear some noise from the restaurant.

"Quick!" Megan whispers. "Someone's coming!"

Ella takes Rosie and puts her back into the rucksack. Megan looks around. There is silence. The restaurant is right next to the Learning Centre, and there is a door between the two buildings. Megan goes to the door and opens it. There is no light in the restaurant, and no sound.

Then there is a sound. It is the sound of a person coming towards the Learning Centre, but this time from the other side of the room. The main door opens. It is Mrs Miller.

"Hello, girls," she says to Megan and Ella. "You're a bit early for the break. And where are the others?"

"They're still with the otters," Ella says. "Or maybe the lions. We don't know."

"Pip's sick, Mum," Megan says. "Tom and the vet are 5 looking after him right now."

"You mean Tom's not with the others?" Mrs Miller asks with wide open eyes. "That's not a good idea!"

"They all want to come back to the restaurant soon, Mrs Miller," Ella says. She is getting a bit nervous now. 10

"Right. Let me have a quick look. I hope they're already back," Mrs Miller says and walks off into the restaurant.

The girls take a deep breath. But suddenly, they can hear a loud scream from the restaurant.

"What was that?" Jeff asks. The boys all look at each other. 15 They are on their way to the Learning Centre, about fifty metres away from the restaurant.

"I think that was my mother," Luke says, looking worried and excited. "What's going on?"

"Maybe the monkey's in the restaurant," Jacob says. 20

"Let's have a look then," Luke says. "Ron, can you go to the Learning Centre and check if everything's OK? And close all doors and windows."

The boys all move towards the restaurant. Ron walks on to the Learning Centre. 25

"Hiya," Ron says when he enters the room. "Are you all right?!" Suddenly, there is a 'screech, screech' sound coming from Ella's rucksack.

"What's that?" Ron asks.

"Nothing," Ella says. Her face is getting red.

"Hey, what's wrong? What do you have in your rucksack?"

The rucksack is moving and suddenly Rosie sticks her head out.

5 Ron cannot believe his eyes.

"Isn't that Rosie, the baby monkey?" he asks. "How can you take her with you? Are you mad?"

He gives both girls an angry look.

"It was her idea!" Megan says and points at Ella.

10 "What?" Ella shouts.

"You can't do that! We have to take Rosie back to the cage. Probably her mother's already looking for her!"

Then Ron stops. Suddenly, lots of things are going through his head.

15 "Hey, Mum, are you all right, is everything OK?" Luke says when he and his friends enter the restaurant.

"Yes, I'm fine, thanks," Mrs Miller says.

"Is the monkey in here?" Jacob asks.

"How do you know there's a monkey in here?" Mrs Miller 20 asks. She looks at Luke.

Luke suddenly feels sick. He looks at Jacob, then at his mother. There is a long moment of silence. But then Luke thinks it is really best to tell her the truth. He takes a deep breath and tells his mother the whole story. Mrs Miller does 25 not interrupt her son. She listens until Luke is finished.

"So now we're all looking for him," Luke says.

"How can you lose a monkey???" Mrs Miller is angry. "Were you in the cage? That's dangerous! Does Tom know? ...

But that's not important at the moment. We have to get Jane back into the cage!"

"Jane?" Luke asks. "Do you mean that monkey is Rosie's mother?"

"Come on, Luke, you know what Jane looks like!" Luke's 5 mother says,

"So where is he now? Oh, I mean she", Jacob asks.

"She's hiding under that table over there," Mrs Miller replies, still angry. "And we have to work together if we want to catch her." 10

"I'm so sorry Mum!" Luke says.

"Let's talk about it later, Luke" says his mother.

Suddenly, the door to the restaurant opens. Luke holds his breath. Then he sighs when he sees Ron.

"Hey, Ron!" Luke shouts. "The monkey's here in the 15 restaurant! And it's a she! It's Jane, Rosie's mother!"

"Yeah," Ron says. "And I think I know what she's looking for."

"I can't believe it girls! What a stupid idea! But let's not talk about it now, we have to catch Jane now!" Mrs Miller 20 says. "First, we're too many people in here. Jane's already scared, anyway. Second, we need to find something to catch her with. A rucksack is too small."

They all go back to the Learning Centre and leave the door to the restaurant open. 25

"OK, we're going to use Rosie to get close to her. Jane is looking for her baby, so it shouldn't be a problem to catch her that way."

"What about this box here?" Malik says. "It looks big enough."

He points to a box next to him and opens it. With a loud scream, he closes it again. He looks scared.

5 "Good idea," Mrs Miller says. "But someone has to hold Suzie, then."

"Not me!" Ella shouts. The other children are looking a bit scared too.

"OK, so that's my job, then," Mrs Miller sighs. "And who's
10 going to take the box and catch Jane?"

"I can try," Ron says and smiles.

Mrs Miller and the children are standing in a far corner of the room. Everyone is quiet. Rosie is sitting in the box.

Ron pushes the box into the restaurant. He is holding
15 Rosie and moving the box towards Jane at the same time. Then he stops. Jane looks at them. She wants to get close to Rosie, but you can see that she is scared.

"Komm her, meine Kleine," Ron says. "Keine Angst, ich tu dir nichts. "

20 "What is he saying?" Ella whispers to Jacob.

"I don't know," Jacob says. "I think he's speaking Monkeyish."

"Monkeyish?"

"Yeah, the monkey language," Jacob says. "Look!"

25 Jane is not looking scared any more. She gets closer and then climbs into the box. Then she grabs Rosie and holds her really close. The two monkeys do not move.

Ron closes the box. Everyone is happy and smiles.

"Erm, Mum," Luke says. "I'm so sorry! I think we all really liked the sleepover, and I'm very sorry about the monkey. But we still can have sleepovers, can't we?" Luke is worried that this could be the end of the sleepover idea. "Well, Luke, for the moment I'm only happy that you and your friends are all right and that we have our monkeys back. But, next time we have to make sure that there is always at least one adult with the children. You and your friends were lucky because you know the zoo. But children who don't know the zoo ... I don't want to think about it ..." 5

10

8 SAYING GOODBYE

Three days later, Luke, Ron and Tom are at the otter pool. It is six o'clock in the evening. The zoo is closed, but the zookeepers still have some work to do.

Pip is back in the pool. He is not sick any more. He is swimming around and playing with the other otters. 15

"I hope that we don't have to see the vet again this summer," Tom says. "It wasn't easy to get Pip back to normal. We had to watch him for a long time. That was when you were all having a good time with the monkeys."

"Sorry, Tom," Luke says and looks down. 20

"Don't worry. There's some good news from the monkeys too. We're going to have another baby monkey soon."

"Really?" Luke shouts. "That's great! But watch out for Megan. She has some funny ideas about baby monkeys."

"Don't worry. I think she knows that it was stupid to take 25 Rosie away from her mother."

"That's right," Luke says. "OK, are we finished? Then let's go. The others should be here now."

At the Learning Centre, the Millers and all the other sleepover children are waiting for Luke, Ron and Tom. Jeff is preparing his video camera and the TV.

"Hi, everyone!" Luke shouts when they enter the room. "Good to see you again!"

"Hey, Ron," Ella says. "That was so cool of you to catch the monkey. You know what? I really want to learn German now. I'm going to take German when I'm in Year 8. Maybe you can help me with it?"

"Maybe," Ron says and smiles back.

"I'm so excited to see what Jeff's film's like!" Jacob says. "Jeff, are you ready?"

"Yes," Jeff replies. "Here we go!"

The video starts. There are some scenes of the zoo in daylight with interesting background music. Then you can hear Jeff's voice.

"Welcome to Stockbridge Zoo. We're not like any other zoo. At Stockbridge Zoo, you can have the time of your life!"

"You sound so cool!" Luke whispers to Jeff.

Now you can see the Learning Centre. There are some scenes of Ella holding Suzie and then screaming.

"You can meet some really dangerous animals," Jeff's voice goes on.

The children start to laugh. Ella just makes a funny face.

The next scenes are at the monkeys' cage. The children are feeding the monkeys. Then you can see the monkey on Jacob's back, and Jacob shouting.

"Get really close to the animals," Jeff's voice says.

Again, the children start to laugh. This time, Jacob stays quiet.

"Fight with the animals," Jeff's voice says, and you can see Jacob jump onto his torch. 5

There are more scenes showing the otters, the elephants and the lions as they are walking around the tree.

"Wildlife at its best," Jeff's voice says. "A sleepover at Stockbridge Zoo – it's going to be the time of your life!"

Everyone claps and cheers. 10

"Brilliant film!" Luke shouts.

"Really good," Mrs Miller says. "But maybe we have to edit one or two scenes before we upload it to our website."

Later, all the sleepover children and Luke's parents are sitting around a large table in the restaurant. They are having 15 some snacks. Mr Miller starts to speak in front of the group.

"So, let me say thank you to all of you," he says. "The test sleepover was very important for us. We had to check if it works. And I think it does. But we have to change a few things ..." 20

"Let me also say thank you to our visitor from Germany, who is going to leave tomorrow," Mr Miller goes on. "Ron, you're a great zookeeper. We hope you had a good time with our animals and we hope to see you again at Stockbridge Zoo soon. And we have a little present for you." 25

Mr Miller hands over the present. Ron opens it. It's a red "SZ" T-shirt and a black cap.

"Welcome to the zoo team!" Luke says, and everyone claps and cheers.

VOCABULARY

Abbreviations
jm., jn. – jemandem, jemanden; pl – Plural;
sb. – somebody; sth. – something

A

about [əˈbaʊt] ungefähr
allowed [əˈlaʊd]: be allowed to do sth.
  etwas tun dürfen
already [ɔːlˈredi] schon, bereits
anyway [ˈeniweɪ]: Anyway, ...
  Jedenfalls ...; ..., anyway sowieso;
  Why ... anyway? Wieso ...
  überhaupt?
(to) appear [əˈpɪə] erscheinen,
  auftauchen
apple [ˈæpl] Apfel
at least [æt, ət ˈliːst] zumindest,
  wenigstens

B

banana [bəˈnɑːnə] Banane
bar [bɑː] (Gitter)stab
beautiful [ˈbjuːtɪfl] schön
(to) begin [bɪˈgɪn] beginnen, anfangen
(to) believe [bɪˈliːv] glauben
bit [bɪt]: a bit ein bisschen, etwas
both [bəʊθ] beide
branch [brɑːntʃ] Ast, Zweig
breath [breθ] Atem, Atemzug
brilliant [ˈbrɪliənt] großartig, genial
building [ˈbɪldɪŋ] Gebäude
bush [bʊʃ] Busch, Gebüsch

C

care [keə(r)]: (to) care (about sth.)
  sich für etwas interessieren

carnival [ˈkɑːnɪvl] Fasching, Karneval
(to) celebrate [ˈselɪbreɪt] feiern
celebrity [səˈlebrəti] Berühmtheit
(to) cheer [tʃɪə] jubeln
chips [tʃɪps] Pommes Frites
(to) clap [klæp] (Beifall) klatschen
costume [ˈkɒstjuːm] Kostüm,
  Verkleidung
could [kʊd, kəd] könnte; konnte
cow [kaʊ] Kuh
cute [kjuːt] süß, niedlich

D

daylight [ˈdeɪlaɪt] Tageslicht
deep [diːp] tief
difficult [ˈdɪfɪkəlt] schwierig, schwer
(to) dress [dres] sich anziehen
(to) drop sth. [drɒp] etwas fallen
  lassen

E

(to) enter [ˈentə(r)] betreten,
  hineingehen in
even [ˈiːvn] sogar; not even (noch)
  nicht einmal
everything [ˈevriθɪŋ] alles

F

few [fjuː]: a few ein paar, einige
fifteen [ˌfɪfˈtiːn] fünfzehn
fifty [ˈfɪfti] fünfzig
free [friː]: for free kostenlos

G

gate [geɪt] Tor, Pforte, Gatter
giant [ˈʤaɪənt] Riese(n)
(to) give up [gɪv_ʌp] aufgeben
going to [ˈgəʊɪŋ_tuː] werden; I'm
  going to do it Ich werde es tun
(to) grab [græb] schnappen, packen
ground [graʊnd] (Erd-)Boden

H

had (to) [həd]: hatte (past tense von
  have (to)
holiday [ˈhɒlədeɪ] Urlaub

I

if [ɪf] wenn, falls; ob
injection [ɪnˈʤekʃn] Spritze
interested [ˈɪntrəstɪd]: be interested
  (in) sich interessieren (für)
(to) interrupt [ˌɪntəˈrʌpt] unterbrechen

J

jealous [ˈʤeləs] neidisch, eifersüchtig

K

key [kiː] Schlüssel
(to) kill [kɪl] töten

L

large [lɑːʤ] groß
(to) lie [laɪ] liegen; he is lying er liegt
  gerade
(to) look forward to sth. [lʊk ˈfɔːwəd]
  sich auf etwas freuen
lucky [ˈlʌki]: be lucky Glück haben

M

magic [ˈmæʤɪk] magisch, Zauber-

make sure that [meɪk ʃʊə, ʃɔː] darauf
  achten, dass
(to) mean [miːn] meinen, sagen wollen
message [ˈmesɪʤ] Nachricht

N

native speaker [ˈneɪtɪv ˈspiːkə]
  Muttersprachler
nearby [ˌnɪəˈbaɪ] nahegelegen
nephew [ˈnefjuː] Neffe
nervous [ˈnɜːvəs] nervös, aufgeregt
next to [nekst] neben
(to) nod [nɒd] nicken
noise [nɔɪz] Krach, Lärm
normal [ˈnɔːml] normal

O

off [ɒf] weg (von), davon; herunter; ab
(to) offer [ˈɒfə(r)] anbieten
older [əʊldə] älter
own [əʊn]: on my/your/their ... own
  allein

P

path [pɑːθ] Pfad, Weg
probably [ˈprɒbəbli] wahrscheinlich
project [ˈprɒʤekt] Projekt

Q

quick [kwɪk] schnell

R

race [reɪs] Rennen
(to) react [riˈækt] reagieren
(to) reply [rɪˈplaɪ] antworten, erwidern;
  he replies er antwortet
reptile [ˈreptaɪl] Reptil
rule [ruːl] Regel

S

safety ['seɪfti] Sicherheit

scared [skeəd]: be scared (of) Angst haben (vor)

(to) scream [skriːm] schreien, kreischen

should [ʃəd]: we should wir sollten

Shush! [ʃʊʃ] Pst!

(to) shut up [ʃʌt_ʌp] den Mund halten

(to) sigh [saɪ] seufzen

silence ['saɪləns] Stille

sleeping bag [sliːpɪŋ bæg] Schlafsack

social media ['səʊʃl 'miːdiə] soziale Medien

son [sʌn] Sohn

spider ['spaɪdə] Spinne

(to) stick [stɪk] stecken

stupid ['stjuːpɪd] bescheuert, blöd, auch: Idiot

such [sʌtʃ] solch, so ein(e)

sunny ['sʌni] sonnig

sure [ʃʊə(r)] sicher

T

temperature ['temprətʃə(r)] Temperatur

text message [tekst 'mesɪdʒ] SMS

torch [tɔːtʃ] Taschenlampe

towards [təˈwɔːdz] in Richtung …

truth [truːθ] Wahrheit

(to) turn to sb. [tɜːn] sich jm. zuwenden

U

(to) unpack [ˌʌnˈpæk] auspacken

until [ənˈtɪl] bis

(to) upload [ˌʌpˈləʊd] hochladen

usual ['juːʒuəl] gewöhnlich

V

vet (veterinary) [vet] Tierarzt

visitor ['vɪzɪtə(r)] Besucher/in, Gast

W

wall [wɔːl] Mauer, Wand

warning ['wɔːnɪŋ] Warnung

way [weɪ]: No way! Auf keinen Fall!

What's up? [wɒt] Was ist los?

(to) whisper ['wɪspə(r)] flüstern

wide [waɪd]: wide open weit geöffnet

wildlife ['waɪldlaɪf] wild lebende Tiere

(to) wink (at sb.) [wɪŋk] jm. zuzwinkern

(to) worry ['wʌri] sich Sorgen machen

CHECK YOUR UNDERSTANDING

Chapter 1: Luke Miller
1 Where is Jeff going to go on holiday?
2 Why doesn't Luke want his classmates to visit the zoo for free?
3 What does Jacob want from Luke?

Chapter 2: A new idea
1 Why is Luke late at the otter pool?
2 Who is going to visit Tom next week?
3 What do the Miller family really think about Megan's idea?

Chapter 3: Tom's nephew
1 Why can't Paul join the sleepover?
2 What is Ron doing at the otter pool?
3 Which animals does Ron not like?

Chapter 4: The big night
1 What is Jeff's new hobby?
2 Who is going to hold Suzie?
3 Why can't Jacob hold Suzie?

Chapter 5: The rhesus monkeys
1 What does the monkey grab from Jacob's rucksack?
2 What does Ella do with Rosie?
3 What's wrong with Pip?

Chapter 6: Going on a safari
1 Where do the children find the monkey?
2 What do Ron and Malik find in the bush?
3 How does the monkey get away from the lions?

Chapter 7: How to catch a monkey
1 Why does Mrs Miller suddenly scream?
2 What is the monkey looking for?
3 How does Ron catch the monkey?

Chapter 8: Saying goodbye
1 What are the sleepover children doing in the Learning Centre?
2 What is the present for Ron?